Contents

Braai equipment   2-3
Food selection, preparation and cooking   4-5
Griddle breakfast   6
Beef fillet treat   8
Sweet-and-sour sparerib braai   10
Spur-of-the-moment spread   12

Traditional grill   14
Chicken barbecue   16
Chunky pork chop braai   18
Oriental pork delight   20
Butterflied lamb   22
Rack of lamb feast   24

Braai equipment

TYPES OF BRAAI

The diversity in braaiing arrangements is marked – from the basic pit filled with burning coals, through all manner of portable braais, to the highly sophisticated built-in arrangement with numerous special features. Whatever the set-up, the method of braaiing is essentially the same and the cooked food always appetizing.

A simple hole in the ground makes a perfectly adequate site for a braai fire, although most people make some effort to create a more structured cooking area – even if it's just a simple grid-on-bricks arrangement, a wheelbarrow or a foil-lined cast-iron pot with a grid. Basic as it may be, a grid on top of bricks is extremely versatile, enabling you to control the heat by adding or removing brick layers to raise or lower the grid.

PORTABLE BRAAIS

Portable braais are ideal for beach picnics or country outings, as they are generally collapsible and easily reassembled. The simplest forms are the disposable braai packs: small, aluminium containers, complete with charcoal, which are thrown away after use. The Hibachi braai consists of a cast-iron 'box' base with vents which can be adjusted to control the rate of burning; it also has an adjustable grid. Perhaps most popular of the portable models are the open braziers which usually have wheels for easy movement. Most have adjustable grids, and some incorporate a half-hood, which protects the fire from the wind.

Kettle braais, such as the Weber, are among the most sophisticated portable braais available. These consist of a large fire bowl (which supports the fire grill and cooking grid) and a removable hood or lid. A single layer of coals is fired on top of the fire grill, and food is laid upon the grid in the *direct* method of cooking. The hood adds another dimension to the braai, serving as a wind break when open and as an oven when closed. The inside of the hood reflects and circulates the heat when it is down, so that food cooks evenly and more rapidly (even than a conventional oven) in what is known as the *indirect* method of cooking. This is ideal for cooking whole chickens and joints of meat. A host of accessories, including a rib-rack, wok, and rotisserie, are available for the Weber kettle, making the braai even more versatile. Although the grid level is fixed, a series of adjustable dampers in the bowl allow for heat control.

Electric outdoor grills, such as the Hot Rock, simulate the braaiing method but without the fuss of building a fire. They cook food quickly and efficiently.

Gas braais are much cleaner and quicker than braais fired by wood or charcoal, and are easily moved under cover if weather conditions take a sudden turn for the worse. Gas can be used with a grid or 'skottel' attachment. The grid is used in the normal way, while the skottel – a concave, round dish, reminiscent of a plough-disc and similar to a Chinese wok – is ideal for stir-frying,

Various braaiing options: built-in braai, a Weber kettle braai (left) and a gas braai with a skottel attachme[nt]

as meat juices and sauces collect in the base and can be used repeatedly for basting.

BUILT-IN BRAAIS

Built-in braais have become increasingly popular. They offer the obvious advantage of a permanent place in which to braai, but lack the flexibility of portable models which can be moved to accommodate changes in weather, particularly wind direction. Therefore, it is extremely important when building a braai to plan carefully and to take into account its location in relation to prevailing winds, so as to avoid smoking out an adjoining patio area or even the house. Most built-in braais have open grids – ideal for cooking steak, chicken, chops, ribs and sausages. These are often adjustable to different levels and can be raised or lowered according to the heat intensity required. Many other useful features can be incorporated into the design for convenience and diversity in cooking: working surfaces, a dry storage area for wood or charcoal; a potjie shelf and attachment; a spit for spit-roasting large joints, a Dutch baking oven, and even a pizza oven, which is effective for both baking and braaiing.

BRAAI UTENSILS

Grids The two types of grid available – flat and hinged – offer different advantages: a flat grid allows you to cook and attend to different cuts of meat individually, and to move meat from hot to cool areas of the braai. Hinged grids are better for cooking large quantities of meat – usually of the same cut and thickness – which do not require individual attention.

A **wire brush** is useful for cleaning the grid of charred leftovers before and after use.

A sturdy pair of long-handled **tongs** is essential for turning meat as it will not pierce the flesh and release the juices. A shorter, scissor-type pair is useful for handling the coals.

A **flameproof apron** will protect cloth[es] from sparks and flames.

A long-handled **basting brush** is handy basting meat with a marinade or oil. D[on't] buy one with plastic bristles as these m[ay] melt from the heat of the fire.

Oven gloves should be padded on both si[des] for added protection against burns cause[d by] splattering and sparking.

Skewers, used for sosaties and kebabs, [can] be metal, wooden or bamboo. Metal skew[ers] may be used over and over again but do t[end] to burn the food closest to them, and [are] tricky to handle when hot. Wooden and b[am]boo skewers overcome these problems [but] can generally be used only once or twice.

A **fire-starter** is a relatively new device wh[ich] is used to stimulate a charcoal fire. The [gal]vanized, bin-like container is packed [half] way up with paper and then topped up w[ith] charcoal. The paper, set alight, serves to [fire] the charcoal, which in minutes is glow[ing] and ready to be transferred to the braai.

Other items which may come in useful aro[und] the braai include a jug of water for quench[ing] rising flames, a platter for stacking cooked f[ood] and a food warmer.

THE FIRE

FUEL

Whatever fuel you choose, don't skimp! [It's] better to err on the generous side than to f[ace] the embarrassment of a dying fire before the food is cooked. Both quality and quant[ity] of coals are important to the success o[f a] braai, so if you are cooking large quantitie[s of] food, it's a good idea to start a second fire[, or] use a fire-starter, to replenish the cooking [fire] with burning coals.

Charcoal can be bought in briquette fo[rm] and in chunks. Briquettes provide an ev[en,] constant heat and burn for a long ti[me.] Chunks of charcoal will light more easily [but] are inclined to 'splutter' and spark.

Wood is a very popular option because the smoke given off imparts a distinctive flavour to the food. Whatever kind of wood you choose to braai with, be sure that it is dry: fresh, green wood lights with difficulty and creates a lot of smoke. Among the most popular wood types for braaiing are leadwood, karee and ironwood, all of which produce hot coals, and hook thorn and boikrans, which create moderate to hot coals. Do not use tamboti or oleander woods which give off poisonous fumes, and avoid gum woods which impart an unpleasant resinous flavour. Never use wood that has been painted or treated in some way. Vine stumps, dried pine cones (particularly useful in starting a fire) and mealie cobs can also be used as fire fuel.

Gas provides an alternative to solid fuel, and is both convenient and reliable, although appropriate equipment is a prerequisite.

BUILDING AND STARTING A FIRE

The simplest way to start a fire is to use crumpled newspaper and twigs (kindling), stacked upright around the paper; light the paper and add more kindling as the fire takes light. Commercial fire-lighters – made of a porous, flammable material and impregnated with paraffin – can be employed to speed up the process, but should be used sparingly and allowed to evaporate completely before the grid is positioned. Once the fire is underway, start adding the solid fuel gradually, and allow it to burn down to form hot coals. Spread the coals out before starting to cook.

WHEN TO BRAAI

Although different cuts of meat require different degrees of heat, there is a particular stage to which the fire should burn before anything is cooked on it: the coals should be hot enough to seal the meat and retain the juices, but not so hot that they burn the food before the inside is cooked. With a charcoal braai, coals should be ready after 30 to 45 minutes, or when they are covered in a fine layer of grey ash. Wood fires generally take longer to burn down, and should have passed the 'flame stage' to form a heap of glowing coals before it is 'safe' to cook. It is important to remember that the depth of the coals affects the heat, also that the central coals are always hotter than those around the edges. The less intense heat at the fire edges is ideal for foil-wrapped vegetables, while meat is best cooked over the hotter centre. Steaks, in particular, require very hot coals and should be cooked over a bed of 100 mm depth; a 50 mm-deep bed is sufficient for most other cuts.

CONTROLLING TEMPERATURE

To change the temperature at which the food is cooking, use one of the following methods:
• raise or lower the grid: the closer the food to the fire, the higher the temperature at which it cooks;
• remove or add coals to reduce or increase heat;
• in the case of a portable braai with dampers (vents), open the vents to raise the temperature and close them to decrease it.

A colourful assortment of braai utensils and accessories

Solid fuel, added after the kindling has taken light, must burn long enough to form hot coals for braaiing.

Food selection, preparation and cooking

MEAT

SELECTING MEAT

Whether it is beef, lamb or pork you intend braaiing, the single most important rule is to buy the best quality meat, as this is usually the most tender and succulent. Less tender cuts should be reserved for the long-cooking process of a potjie meal. The following cuts are most suitable and make the most successful braais:

Beef Choose prime rib, wing rib, club steak, Scotch fillet, rib-eye, sirloin, T-bone steak, entrecote steak, porterhouse steak, rump steak or fillet steak. Steak should be no less than 25-30 mm thick, except porterhouse which for best results should be thicker, about 50 mm. Short rib and flat rib, although not as tender as those already mentioned, are very tasty and especially flavoursome when marinated.

Always buy fresh, quality beef, which is cherry red in colour with a firm, smooth texture. The fat should be firm and white and evenly distributed, cartilage white, soft and elastic, and sawn bones surfaces should appear red and porous. Do not buy meat with a lot of sinew.

Lamb Chops from the rib, loin and chump should be you first choice. Thick rib and leg chops are also suitable. All should be 20-25 mm thick. Saddle of lamb, breast ribs, noisettes and cutlets are also good for braaiing.

Buy fresh, quality lamb with a bright pink colour and a firm, smooth texture. Otherwise, the same criteria apply for fat, cartilage and bones as those stated for beef.

Pork The same cuts as those for lamb are best for braaiing, with the addition of pork spareribs, which are delicious braaied.

Pork meat should have a greyish pink appearance and, like beef and lamb, its texture should be firm and smooth. The same criteria for fat, cartilage and bones apply.

PREPARING MEAT

Clean the meat with a cloth moistened with vinegar and cut away any surplus fat. Slash the edges of the remaining fat to prevent the meat curling during cooking. If you are braaiing marinated pork, remove the rind and cook it separately to crisp it. Pat the meat dry with a paper towel.

Season the meat with herbs of your choice. Do not add salt at this stage as it will make the meat tough and dry; instead, add it towards the end of the cooking period or once the meat is cooked.

Marinades, made up of one part oil, two parts acid (vinegar, lemon juice, wine) and selected seasonings, add a special verve to braaied meat. They also prevent drying out and help to tenderize tougher cuts. For best results allow the meat to marinate (turning once) for at least 2 hours, often longer depending on the type and cut. It is also important to baste the meat with the marinade during the cooking process. Meat most suited to marinating includes all pork cuts, breast of lamb, and beef, lamb and pork ribs, which are greatly enhanced by the marinade flavour. Sausages should not be marinated.

COOKING MEAT

Meat can be cooked on a braai in a variety of ways, most common of which is on a open grid over a bed of coals. Chops, ribs, sausages, kebabs and steaks are best done this way, absorbing as they cook the fire's smoke to produce that matchless 'braai flavour'. With the exception of beef steaks, which require fast cooking over very hot coals, all meat should be cooked over a *moderately* hot fire.

Cooking under a hood Larger pieces of meat, such as whole Scotch fillet and lamb and pork joints, are best cooked under a hood – ideally that of a kettle braai. If you don't have such a braai, you can simulate the cooking method by constructing a domed wire framework and covering it with foil, or by placing an inverted heat-proof bowl over the meat. The hood method reduces the cooking time by trapping heat and circulating it, so that the meat cooks from all sides. When cooking in this way, always brown the joint over an open fire first, then cover with the hood. Because a lot of fat drips from the meat in cooking, arrange the coals around the edges of the fire area and place a dish in the centre beneath the meat to catch the fat. Baste regularly with meat juices to prevent drying out.

Stir-frying is most successfully done on a skottel braai. The cooking process is very quick and the results delicious. Slivers of meat, especially pork which has been marinated, are ideal for stir-frying.

Spit-roasting A whole lamb or pig, cooked over a fire on a spit, is invariably a hit, especially for a large party. The cooking process is a long one (lamb: 5-7 hours, pig: 7-9 hours) and is usually carried out on an electric or mechanical spit. You can, however, construct you own spit using a sturdy, clean rod and pole supports. The coals for cooking a lamb or pig must be red hot but must not be allowed flame. Because of the long cooking process, 'reserve' fires should be made to replenish the cooking fire as it burns down.

Foil-wrap Cooking in foil is more like steaming than braaiing and the method is better suited to vegetables than meat, although pork can be successfully cooked in this way. Because the foil seals completely, it traps all moisture and flavour within the package. Always use heavy duty foil, shiny side facing inwards, and remember to oil it to prevent the food from sticking.

Top right: Beef cuts (left to right): wing rib, T-bone, rump, rib-eye, club, porterhouse, fillet.

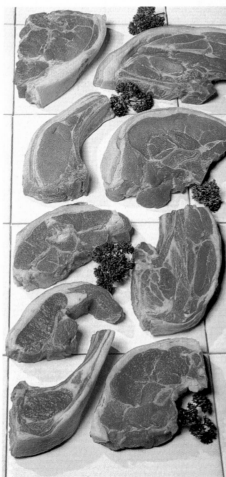

Bottom right: (left to right) Pork cuts: loin, shoulder (braai chop) cutlet, chump; Lamb cuts: saddle, shoulder (braai chop), loin, cutlet, chump.

HICKEN

LECTING CHICKEN

chicken with pink, firm flesh and creamy
ured skin, and avoid birds with a greyish
earance. If you are buying pre-packed
ken, make sure that there is no pink
id in the pack – a sign that the chicken
been frozen, allowed to defrost and fro-
again. Smell is also a good guide to
hness.

EPARING CHICKEN

ole chicken Remove the plastic bag con-
ing the giblets from the cavity, and check
all feathers and bristles have been prop-
removed. Trim off any excess skin and
off the tips of the wings to prevent
ring in cooking. Rinse chicken well and
dry with a paper towel.

hole chicken can be seasoned, inside and
or filled with stuffing. It can also be
tterflied': cut through the breast bones
spread the carcass flat, then push a clean,
stick through from the neck to the par-
's nose.

ed chicken can be used for kebabs,
ich make a mouth-watering treat when
chicken is skewered alternately with
ons, button mushrooms, cherry tomatoes,
ruit chunks.

ered chicken is ideal for stir-frying, and
be combined with julienne vegetables
tangy sauces.

OKING CHICKEN

not salt chicken until cooked, as salt tends to
it out.

ole chicken: cooks very successfully in a
le braai. It is also tasty spit-roasted, but
take 1 – 1½ hours to cook this way.

terflied whole chicken: braai on an open
over moderate coals, turning often and
ting with oil or marinade.

cken portions are generally braaied on
open grid over moderate coals, and will
k fairly quickly if they have been pre-
mered. Baste with oil or marinade
ughout the cooking period. Turn them
uently and, once the skins have
wned, move them to a cooler part of the

EGETABLES AND
RUIT

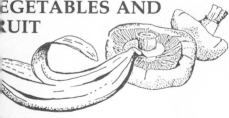

LECTION

atoes, onions, mushrooms, tomatoes,
njals, squash and mealies all cook well on
raai. Fruit suitable for braaiing includes
eapples, bananas, prunes, and dried apri-

cots and peaches. Always ensure that fresh
fruit and vegetables are ripe but still firm.

PREPARING AND COOKING

Whole brinjals cooked, uncovered, over a
fire, are delicious. Mealies in their husks, as
well as unpeeled bananas, cook perfectly
when placed directly in the coals.

Foil-wrap is almost synonymous with fruit
and vegetables at a braai. Whole, foil-
wrapped potatoes, gems, butternut squash
and onions, for instance, are commonly
placed directly in the coals around the edge
of the fire. Remember to prick the skins of
these first three with a fork, to prevent them
from splitting, before wrapping them in a
double thickness of foil with the shiny side
facing inwards. Onions should be left in their
skins rather than peeled.

Pineapples, halved lengthways, can be
wrapped in foil and braaied over moderate
coals; served with whipped cream or ice-
cream, they make a delightful end to the
meal.

Foil can also be used very effectively in
making mixed vegetable parcels. Cut the vegetables into equal-sized pieces, season to
taste and dot with butter before wrapping up
in individual parcels.

Skewered fruit and vegetables are also popular braaied. Onions, tomatoes, brinjals,
mushrooms, mealies, pineapple and dried
fruit are the best ingredients, and the kebabs
should be cooked over a moderate fire.

Remember to parboil onions before cooking
them in this way. Dried fruit should be
presoaked for at least 30 minutes before
skewering. Fruit kebabs can be basted, while
braaiing, with honey or fruit juice for extra
flavour.

Other ideas Some fruit (fresh peaches and
apricots in particular) and vegetables (peppers, tomatoes and brinjals) taste wonderful
when filled with tasty stuffings and braaied
on an open grid over a moderate fire. Peeled
bananas, halved and then wrapped in bacon
secured with a toothpick, can be cooked in
the same way.

Spit-roasting a whole lamb will take up to seven hours, but the results are well worth waiting for.

Marinades, made with oil, vinegar or wine, and a variety of herbs and spices, add zest to braaied meat.

Griddle breakfast

Breakfast prepared outdoors is a great weekend or holiday treat, and is a novel way to entertain. All your favourite delicacies, including grapefruit, can be prepared in the skottelbraai or on a griddle over the coals.

MENU *Serves six*
Grilled grapefruit
Liver, kidney and bacon medley
Fried eggs
Crunchy mealie fritters
Jams and whole preserves

Grilled grapefruit

Heat a skottelbraai or griddle. Halve 3 grapefruit and place them, cut side down, on the heated surface for 2 to 3 minutes, or until hot. Sprinkle with brown sugar mixed with a little ground cinnamon or ginger. Serve immediately.

Liver, kidney and bacon medley

750 g calf's, lamb's or chicken liver
6 rashers bacon
10 ml (2 teaspoons) margarine or sunflower oil
1 large onion, sliced
6 calf's or sheep's kidneys, cleaned and halved
5 ml (1 teaspoon) salt
10 ml (2 teaspoons) cornflour
125 ml (½ cup) red wine

Heat a skottelbraai or griddle. Cut liver into strips and set aside. Fry bacon for 2 to 3 minutes or until fat becomes transparent. Add margarine or oil and allow to heat through. Add onion and sauté until transparent. Add liver and kidneys and, stirring regularly, allow meat to cook for about 10 minutes or until tender. Season with salt. Mix cornflour and wine until smooth, and stir into meat medley. Cook for 5 minutes or until sauce thickens. Keep mixture warm until ready to serve.

Fried eggs

Fry eggs on the griddle in a little melted margarine or butter.

Crunchy mealie fritters

250 ml (1 cup) bread flour
2 eggs
125 ml (½ cup) milk
125 ml (½ cup) cream
500 ml (2 cups) canned whole-kernel corn, drained
125 ml (½ cup) finely chopped fresh chives or spring onions
125 ml (½ cup) grated mature Cheddar cheese
30 ml (2 tablespoons) sunflower oil

Sift flour into a bowl. Whisk eggs, milk and cream together, and beat into flour to make a smooth batter. Stir in corn, chives or spring onions, and cheese. Heat oil in a skottelbraai and, when hot, drop large spoonfuls of batter onto the griddle. Fry on both sides until golden, about 5 to 8 minutes. Serve, buttered, with jam and whole preserves.
(Makes about 30 small fritters)

HINT

● *As with all breakfasts, co-ordination is all-important: grill and serve the grapefruit first; then cook the liver, kidney and bacon medley, and keep it warm while you prepare the fritters. Unless you have a large, flat griddle, these should be cooked separately. Fry the eggs last.*

Beef fillet treat

A marvellously simple way to prepare a spectacular meal.

MENU *Serves six to eight*
Marinated beef fillet
with
Green peppercorn sauce &
Mustard sauce
Onion, mushroom and baby mealie kebabs
Wholewheat bread
Green salad

Marinated beef fillet

1,5–2 kg beef fillet
Marinade
125 ml (½ cup) sunflower oil
125 ml (½ cup) red wine
2 cloves garlic, crushed
5 ml (1 teaspoon) finely chopped fresh rosemary or
** 2 ml (½ teaspoon) dried**
10 ml (2 teaspoons) finely chopped fresh thyme or
** 5 ml (1 teaspoon) dried**
5 ml (1 teaspoon) salt
freshly ground black pepper to taste

Place meat in a large, shallow dish. Mix all marinade ingredients together and pour over meat. Marinate for 30 minutes, turning once. Remove meat from marinade and pat dry with a paper towel. Seal meat by placing it on a braai grid over hot coals. Turn often to ensure that sides are evenly browned. Then, to reduce heat, raise grid or

remove some of the coals, and continue to braai meat, turning a basting it with marinade every 10 minutes. For rare meat, cook for to 35 minutes, and for medium-rare meat, cook for about 40 minute Allow an extra 5 to 10 minutes for meat that is well-done. Carve fi into 1 cm-thick slices and serve with prepared sauces.

Green peppercorn sauce

30 ml (2 tablespoons) cake flour
10 ml (2 teaspoons) mustard powder
10 ml (2 teaspoons) canned green peppercorns, drained
5 ml (1 teaspoon) brown sugar
125 ml (½ cup) chicken or beef stock
250 ml (1 cup) fresh or sour cream or natural yoghurt
5 ml (1 teaspoon) whisky

Place flour, mustard powder, peppercorns and sugar in a sm saucepan. Add stock and stir well. Heat mixture and bring to boil a few minutes, stirring continuously. Remove from heat and stir cream or yoghurt, then add whisky. Serve hot with braaied fillet.

(Makes about 500 ml)

Mustard sauce

4 eggs
75 ml (5 tablespoons) sugar
30 ml (2 tablespoons) mustard powder
15 ml (1 tablespoon) cake flour
2 ml (½ teaspoon) salt
2 ml (½ teaspoon) freshly ground black pepper
250 ml (1 cup) red wine vinegar
10 ml (2 teaspoons) prepared grainy mustard

Beat eggs with 60 ml (4 tablespoons) of the sugar in a mixing bo then set aside. Place remaining sugar in a saucepan, and

...ustard powder, flour, salt and pepper. Add vinegar and then stir ... the beaten egg mixture. Place saucepan over gentle heat and stir ...ntinuously until sauce thickens. Remove from heat and stir in ...repared mustard. Serve hot with braaied fillet.
(Makes about 300 ml)

Green salad

Toss bite-sized pieces of salad greens — oak and butter lettuce, curly endive — into a salad bowl with whole cherry tomatoes, chopped spring onions, green pepper rings and sliced cucumber. Serve with an olive oil and lemon juice dressing.

Onion, mushroom and baby mealie kebabs

- baby onions
- baby mealies, halved
- fresh button mushrooms
- ...0 g butter or garlic butter
- wooden skewers

...rboil onions and mealies. When cool, thread alternate portions of ...ions, mealies and mushrooms onto the skewers. Brush with melted ...tter or garlic butter, and grill over hot coals for about 5 to 8 minutes, ... until cooked through but not too soft.

--- HINTS ---

- *Remember to allow time for the meat to marinate. Make use of this time to prepare the sauces and salad.*
- *It is best to undercook the meat and keep it warm in a heated container. Individual tastes can then be catered for by cooking single slices to the desired degree of 'doneness'.*
- *Place the vegetable kebabs over the fire about 8 minutes before the meat is ready.*
- *The mustard sauce may be reheated, but should not be allowed to boil. It will keep well in the refrigerator for up to a week.*

Wholewheat bread

- ...0 g (4 cups) wholewheat flour
- ...0 ml (1 cup) rolled oats or crushed wheat
- ... ml (2 teaspoons) bicarbonate of soda
- ...ml (1 teaspoon) salt
- ...5 ml (½ cup) milk
- ... ml (1 tablespoon) honey
- ...0 ml (2 cups) natural yoghurt

...ix flour, oats or wheat, bicarbonate of soda and salt together in a ...rge bowl. Warm milk and honey over gentle heat, remove from ...ove and stir in yoghurt. Add to flour mixture, stirring well to form ...sticky dough. Spoon dough into a well-greased loaf tin and bake ...180 °C for 1 hour, or until bread sounds hollow when tapped.

Sweet-and-sour sparerib braai

Tangy beef spareribs are offset by the fresh taste of tropical fruits and crisp julienne vegetables, while griddle cakes, served with fruit butters, complete the subtle blend of flavours.

MENU *Serves six*
Sweet-and-sour beef spareribs
with
sliced tropical fruits
Julienne vegetable parcels
Griddle cakes
with
Assorted fruit butters

Sweet-and-sour beef spareribs

1,5 kg beef spareribs, washed and trimmed
Marinade
125 ml (½ cup) soy sauce
30 ml (2 tablespoons) honey
15 ml (1 tablespoon) sherry
1 clove garlic, crushed

Place spareribs in a shallow baking dish. Mix all marinade ingredients together well, and pour into dish over spareribs. Marinate for 1 hour, then turn meat and marinate for a further hour. Drain, reserving marinade. Braai spareribs over medium coals for 25 to 30 minutes, basting regularly with the marinade.

Serve with a medley of sliced tropical fruits: ripe mangoes, pawpaw, Kiwi fruit and pineapple, arranged attractively on a flat platter.

Julienne vegetable parcels

6 medium carrots
6 medium baby marrows
6 stalks celery
salt and freshly ground black pepper to taste
10 ml (2 teaspoons) finely chopped fresh tarragon or 5 ml (1 teaspoon) dried
butter

Trim and clean all vegetables, then cut up into equal-sized matchstick pieces. Divide vegetable sticks equally between six squares of foil, shiny side facing inwards. Season with salt and pepper, and sprinkle with tarragon. Dot each parcel with butter and fold up securely. Place parcels among coals around edge of fire, where heat is not too intense, and cook for 10 to 15 minutes.

Griddle cakes

250 ml (1 cup) wholewheat flour
250 ml (1 cup) cake flour
15 ml (1 tablespoon) baking powder
2 ml (½ teaspoon) salt
500 ml (2 cups) milk
125 ml (½ cup) sunflower oil
30 ml (2 tablespoons) molasses or honey
3 eggs, separated

Combine flour, baking powder and salt in a bowl. Beat milk, oil, molasses or honey, and egg yolks together. Add to dry ingredients and blend well to form a smooth batter.

Using a clean, dry bowl, beat egg whites until stiff, and fold into batter. Drop tablespoonfuls of batter onto a moderately hot, well-greased skottelbraai or griddle, and cook on both sides until golden, about 5 to 8 minutes. Serve hot with apple, raisin or apricot butter.

(Makes about 16 cakes)

Apple butter

125 ml (½ cup) puréed stewed apples
ground cinnamon to taste
100 g butter, softened

Mix all ingredients thoroughly and refrigerate until needed.

Raisin butter

125 ml (½ cup) seedless raisins or sultanas
125 ml (½ cup) brandy
100 g butter, softened

Soak raisins or sultanas in brandy for about 1 hour or until plump, then purée with any left-over brandy. Blend puréed fruit with butter and refrigerate until needed.

Apricot butter

125 ml (½ cup) stewed dried apricots
10 ml (2 teaspoons) honey
100 g butter, softened

Purée apricots with honey, then blend well with butter. Refrigerate until needed.

(Each recipe makes about 200 ml fruit butter)

HINTS
- *You will need a large braai with griddle, or a standard grid and separate skottel for this menu.*
- *Allow 2 hours for marinating the meat. During this time, the griddle cake mixture and the butters can be prepared.*
- *Remember to place the vegetable parcels in the coals about 10 to 15 minutes before the meat is ready.*

Spur-of-the-moment spread

The advantage of this braai is that it takes so little on-the-spot preparation: the hamburger patties can be prepared in large quantities well ahead of time, and then frozen – interleaved with and wrapped in plastic – until needed. With tasty stuffed sausages, they provide a truly appetizing meal, which will be ready in an instant.

MENU *Serves six*
Hamburgers
Grilled sausages with prune and apricot stuffing

Hamburgers

750 g minced lean beef
1 egg
1 medium onion, finely chopped
1 clove garlic, crushed
7 ml (1½ teaspoons) salt
2 ml (½ teaspoon) freshly ground black pepper
5 ml (1 teaspoon) finely chopped fresh parsley or 2 ml (½ teaspoon) dried
30 ml (2 tablespoons) dry breadcrumbs
6 soft hamburger rolls, halved

Mix all hamburger ingredients thoroughly, and form into 6 large patties. Braai over moderate coals for 3 to 5 minutes on each side. Place rolls, cut side down, on grid and toast briefly over the coals, then assemble hamburgers, adding a selection of the following garnishes:

thickly sliced tomato
thickly sliced onion
lettuce leaves
sliced Cheddar, mozzarella or Blaauwkrantz cheese
green pepper rings
tomato sauce, chutney or prepared mustard

VARIATION
Coat hamburger patties with one or more of the following before braaiing: crushed black peppercorns; crushed coriander; herbed dry breadcrumbs. Press well onto the meat and refrigerate for 1 hour, or place in the freezer for 30 minutes to firm up.
For an exciting Turkish variation, mince the prepared hamburger mixture once more and press tightly into sausage-shaped fricadels. Thread onto metal skewers and place in the freezer for 30 minutes to an hour. Braai quickly on all sides over moderate coals, and serve with spicy sauces.

Grilled sausages with prune and apricot stuffing

6 thick pork sausages
12 pitted prunes, soaked in water or brandy until plump
12 dried apricots, soaked in water or brandy until plump
6 long rashers bacon

Cut a slit in the side of each sausage and prick skin. Place 2 prunes and 2 dried apricots in each slit, and wrap each sausage in a bacon rasher. Secure with a toothpick. Braai sausages over moderate coals, turning regularly, for about 10 to 15 minutes or until cooked through. Serve immediately.

HINTS
- It is wise to brush the grid, skottelbraai or griddle with oil to prevent the patties from sticking.
- If using one of the patty variations, remember to allow for up to 1 hour for refrigeration, which will make the meat easier to handle on the grid.

Traditional grill

This braai has all the elements of a traditional South African event – and proves that the fare doesn't have to be fancy to taste fantastic.

MENU *Serves six*
Sosaties
Farm-style boerewors
Stywe pap or krummel pap
with
Tomato and onion sauce
Spinach salad

Sosaties

1 kg leg of lamb, deboned and cubed
1 kg pork, cubed
250 g dried apricots or peaches
125 ml (½ cup) mutton fat, cubed
12 baby onions or 3 medium onions, quartered

Marinade

75 ml (5 tablespoons) smooth apricot jam
30 ml (2 tablespoons) brown sugar
3 cloves garlic, crushed
15 ml (1 tablespoon) cornflour
2 bay leaves
30 ml (2 tablespoons) curry powder
30 ml (2 tablespoons) red wine vinegar
15 ml (1 tablespoon) salt
5 ml (1 teaspoon) freshly ground black pepper

Place lamb and pork cubes in a shallow dish. Combine all marinade ingredients in a saucepan, stir together, and cook over moderate heat until slightly thickened. Remove from heat and pour over meat cubes. Cover and set aside in a cool place for 4 hours, turning the meat 3 to 4 times to ensure even marinating. Soak apricots or peaches separately in water until plump, then drain. Remove meat from marinade and thread onto skewers alternating with mutton fat, apricots or peaches, and whole baby onions or onion quarters. Braai on all sides over moderate coals for 15 to 20 minutes, basting regularly with the marinade.

VARIATION
Replace lamb with 1 kg cubed chicken.

Farm-style boerewors

60 ml (4 tablespoons) coriander seeds
1,5 kg beef, minced
1,5 kg pork, minced
500 g pork speck, diced
15 ml (1 tablespoon) salt
5 ml (1 teaspoon) freshly ground black pepper
2 ml (½ teaspoon) grated nutmeg
2 ml (½ teaspoon) ground cloves
1 ml (¼ teaspoon) ground allspice
125 ml (½ cup) brown vinegar
1 clove garlic, crushed
45 ml (3 tablespoons) Worcestershire sauce
100 g sausage casing

Dry-roast coriander in a non-stick frying pan, then grind in a pepper mill. Combine well with meat and all remaining ingredients, except sausage casing, to form a crumbly meat mixture. Fill sausage casing with meat mixture, taking care to distribute the fat evenly throughout. Do not pack meat in too tightly. Braai over moderate coals, turning regularly, for 15 to 30 minutes, or until cooked through.

(Makes 3,5-4 kg)

Stywe pap

10 ml (2 teaspoons) salt
1 litre (4 cups) boiling water
500 ml (2 cups) unsifted mealie meal
125 ml (½ cup) cold water

Add salt to boiling water in a cast-iron pot. Pour in mealie meal, cove with lid and leave to simmer over moderate coals for 45 minutes to a hour. Remove lid, stir with a fork and add the cold water. Cover agai and simmer for a further hour or until pap is at desired consistenc Serve with tomato and onion sauce.

Krummel pap

5 ml (1 teaspoon) salt
250 ml (1 cup) water
500 ml (2 cups) coarse yellow mealie meal
250 ml (1 cup) canned whole-kernel corn, drained

Add salt to water and bring to the boil. Sprinkle mealie meal int water and leave to boil for 15 minutes. Stir with a fork to obtain crumbly consistency. Add corn and allow to simmer, partially co ered, for 30 minutes. Serve with tomato and onion sauce.

omato and onion sauce

kg tomatoes, skinned, quartered and seeded
ml (3 tablespoons) sunflower oil
nedium onions, finely chopped
ml (4 tablespoons) finely chopped fresh parsley
ml (2 teaspoons) sugar
nl (1 teaspoon) salt
nl (1 teaspoon) freshly ground black pepper

ce tomatoes in a large saucepan and simmer over low heat until
t and mushy. Meanwhile, heat oil in a frying pan and sauté onion
d parsley over low heat until onion is transparent. Stir in cooked
natoes, sugar, salt and pepper. Cover tightly and simmer for 10 to
minutes. Serve with stywe or krummel pap.

akes 250-300 ml)

Spinach salad

250 g young spinach leaves, washed and broken into bite-sized pieces
125 g feta cheese, cubed
100 g black olives
30 g pine kernels
handful bean sprouts
60 ml (4 tablespoons) vinaigrette dressing

Toss spinach, cheese, olives and pine kernels together in a bowl and
top with bean sprouts. Pour dressing over or allow each person to add
their own.

--- HINTS ---
- *Allow plenty of time for preparation, and double up on meat quantities so as to provide a portion for the freezer.*
- *Pine kernels are very expensive and can be substituted with sunflower seeds, toasted sesame seeds or finely chopped walnuts in the spinach salad.*

Chicken barbecue

Everyone loves a chicken braai which, with tangy sauces and luscious braaied vegetables as accompaniments, becomes a veritable feast.

MENU *Serves six*
Glazed chicken
Peri-peri sauce
Chutney mayonnaise
Mealies in their husks with herbed butter
Braaied tomatoes and brinjals
Garlic toast
Peaches with fruity nut stuffing

Glazed chicken

3 x 1 kg chickens, halved
Marinade
1 medium onion, finely chopped
2 cloves garlic, crushed
15 ml (1 tablespoon) honey
60 ml (4 tablespoons) Worcestershire sauce
15 ml (1 tablespoon) lemon juice
5 ml (1 teaspoon) paprika
45 ml (3 tablespoons) sunflower oil
5 ml (1 teaspoon) Aromat or Fondor

Place halved chickens in a large flat dish. Mix all marinade ingredients together, pour over chicken halves and leave to marinate for 1 to 2 hours, turning once or twice. Remove chicken and pat dry with a paper towel. Braai over moderate coals for 45 minutes to an hour, turning and basting them regularly with the marinade. Serve with peri-peri sauce and chutney mayonnaise.

Peri-peri sauce

30 ml (2 tablespoons) butter
15 ml (1 tablespoon) cornflour
1 medium onion, chopped
1 small chilli, finely chopped
375 ml (1½ cups) chicken stock

Melt butter in a saucepan over gentle heat, then add cornflour and stir until smooth. Remove from heat. Mix onion with chilli and chicken stock, and stir into cornflour mixture. Return saucepan to heat and simmer, stirring constantly, until thickened. Keep warm over cool fire.

Chutney mayonnaise

Mix 250 ml (1 cup) mayonnaise with 60 ml (4 tablespoons) fruit chutney.

Mealies in their husks with herbed butter

6 mealies in their husks
Herbed butter
200 g butter, softened
15 ml (1 tablespoon) finely chopped fresh parsley or
  7 ml (1½ teaspoons) dried
15 ml (1 tablespoon) finely chopped fresh chives or
  7 ml (1½ teaspoons) dried
15 ml (1 tablespoon) finely chopped spring onions
10 ml (2 teaspoons) lemon juice
2 ml (½ teaspoon) salt
freshly ground black pepper to taste

Mix all ingredients for herbed butter thoroughly, and then chill for hour. Peel back (but do not remove) outer husks, and remove sil threads from cobs. Soak cobs in water for 10 minutes. Spread half th herbed butter over the corn and fold husks back to cover the cob Wrap each cob in foil, shiny side facing inwards, and braai over h coals for 15 to 20 minutes, turning often to ensure even cookin Remove cobs from foil, peel off husks and serve with remaini herbed butter.

Braaied tomatoes and brinjals

Wrap 6 ripe, but firm, tomatoes in foil and place on grid together wi 6 small brinjals (uncovered). Cook over cooler edges of fire for 30 to minutes, turning regularly to ensure that all sides are cooked.

Garlic toast

Lightly toast 6 thick slices (2 cm) of French bread over medium co Rub each slice liberally with a piece of garlic and drizzle with go quality olive oil. Serve piping hot.

16

eaches with fruity nut stuffing

pe, but firm, peaches
ml (1 cup) fruit mince
ml ($\frac{1}{2}$ cup) finely chopped walnuts or hazelnuts
ml (1 tablespoon) lemon juice
sh cream, whipped (optional)

lve and stone peaches. Place cut side down on grid and grill lightly
r medium coals. Combine fruit mince, nuts and lemon juice and
on into peach centres. Serve immediately with whipped cream.

——— HINTS ———
Prepare larger quantities of herbed butter and chill. Cut into patties and store
the freezer — interleaved with and wrapped in plastic — for up to 2 months.
e on steaks, potatoes and freshly baked bread.
It is best to use fresh herbs to make the herbed butter.

Chunky pork chop braai

Tender, succulent pork chops filled with a herbed bread stuffing, and served with an unusual choice of salads make the perfect summer-time braai. Round off the meal with delicious fruity kebabs.

MENU *Serves six*

Stuffed pork chops
Patty-pan squash with chive dressing
Peas and tomatoes with mint dressing
Fruit skewers with honey lemon marinade

Stuffed pork chops

6 thick pork chops, trimmed
Herbed bread stuffing
500 ml (2 cups) stale breadcrumbs
125 ml (½ cup) finely chopped celery
1 medium onion, finely chopped
1 clove garlic, crushed
60 ml (4 tablespoons) roasted pine kernels or toasted sesame seeds or finely chopped hazelnuts
60 ml (4 tablespoons) finely chopped fresh dill or 30 ml (2 tablespoons) dried
60 ml (4 tablespoons) finely chopped fresh mint or 30 ml (2 tablespoons) dried
30 ml (2 tablespoons) finely chopped fresh parsley or 15 ml (1 tablespoon) dried
30 g butter, melted
Mustard butter
60 g butter, melted
30 ml (2 tablespoons) prepared mustard
15 ml (1 tablespoon) lemon juice
5 ml (1 teaspoon) finely chopped fresh rosemary or 5 ml (1 teaspoon) dried

Cut deep pockets into each chop. Mix stuffing ingredients together well, and spoon into each pocket. Bring meat around stuffing and secure with toothpick. Combine ingredients for mustard butter, beat well to obtain a smooth consistency, and brush liberally over each chop. Braai chops over moderate coals until tender, about 35 to 40 minutes, turning and basting them often with mustard butter.

Patty-pan squash with chive dressing

1 kg mixed green and yellow patty-pan squash, quartered
125 g ham, chopped
2 apples, cored and sliced
Chive dressing
75 ml (5 tablespoons) cream
60 ml (4 tablespoons) mayonnaise
15 ml (1 tablespoon) chopped fresh chives

Boil, steam or microwave patty-pan squash until just tender. Drain and rinse under cold running water. Pat dry and combine with ham and apples in a bowl. Place dressing ingredients in a screw-top jar, shake well, and pour over salad. Toss lightly to coat.

Peas and tomatoes with mint dressing

750 ml (3 cups) fresh or frozen baby peas
1 English cucumber

4 large spring onions, chopped
250 g whole cherry tomatoes
Mint dressing
125 ml (½ cup) sunflower oil
60 ml (4 tablespoons) white wine vinegar
15 ml (1 tablespoon) finely chopped fresh mint
1 clove garlic, crushed

Boil, steam or microwave peas until just tender. Drain, rinse under cold running water and drain again. Halve cucumber lengthwise, remove seeds, and slice thinly. Place peas, cucumber, onions and tomatoes in a bowl. Combine dressing ingredients in a screw-top jar, shake well and pour over salad. Toss lightly to coat.

Fruit skewers with honey lemon marinade

1 small pineapple, cubed
2 large, ripe bananas, cut into chunks
1 x 410 g can pitted black cherries
1 small orange, peeled and segmented
2 Kiwi fruit, cut into thick slices
60 ml (4 tablespoons) lemon juice
45 ml (3 tablespoons) melted honey
6 wooden skewers

Thread combinations of fruit chunks onto skewers. Mix lemon juice and honey and pour into shallow dish. Marinate fruit in mixture for 30 minutes, turning once. Drain and reserve marinade. Braai fruit skewers on all sides over moderate coals for about 10 minutes or until hot, turning and basting regularly with reserved marinade.

HINTS
● *Prepare the herbed bread stuffing and salad dressings ahead of time to make your task lighter.*
● *Use fresh, rather than dried herbs for the herbed bread stuffing.*

Oriental pork delight

The best of Oriental delights – spicy pork kebabs with sambals, followed by a delectable fruit dessert.

MENU *Serves six*
Satay pork skewers
Spicy peanut sauce
Quince sambal
Apricot sambal
Baked bananas with rum sauce

Satay pork skewers

1 kg boneless lean pork, cubed
Coating
1 small onion, finely chopped
small piece root ginger, peeled and crushed
1 clove garlic, crushed
5 ml (1 teaspoon) fennel seeds
5 ml (1 teaspoon) ground coriander
1 red chilli, finely chopped or 4 drops Tabasco sauce
5 ml (1 teaspoon) salt
Baste
125 ml ($\frac{1}{2}$ cup) sunflower oil mixed with 60 ml (4 tablespoons) lemon juice

Mix all coating ingredients together well. Roll meat in coating mixture, making sure that all pieces are completely covered. Thread cubes onto skewers and grill over moderate coals for about 15 minutes, or until tender. Turn and baste often with oil and lemon juice. Serve with steamed rice and spicy peanut sauce.

Spicy peanut sauce

250 ml (1 cup) crunchy peanut butter
2 cloves garlic, crushed
5 ml (1 teaspoon) peeled and crushed root ginger
1 ml ($\frac{1}{4}$ teaspoon) ground cardamom
1 ml ($\frac{1}{4}$ teaspoon) ground cumin
2 ml ($\frac{1}{2}$ teaspoon) Tabasco sauce
2 ml ($\frac{1}{2}$ teaspoon) paprika
250 ml (1 cup) natural yoghurt

Place all ingredients in a small saucepan, stir well and cook o moderate heat until hot, but not boiling.

Quince sambal

2 ripe quinces
15 ml (1 tablespoon) lemon juice
2 ml ($\frac{1}{2}$ teaspoon) Tabasco sauce
2 ml ($\frac{1}{2}$ teaspoon) salt

Peel and core quinces and grate the flesh coarsely. Sprinkle w lemon juice and mix lightly with Tabasco sauce and salt.

(Makes 250 ml)

Apricot sambal

500 g dried apricots, soaked in water for 1 hour or until plump
25 ml (5 teaspoons) water
25 ml (5 teaspoons) lemon juice
sugar to taste
5 ml (1 teaspoon) ground mixed spice
5 ml (1 teaspoon) finely chopped fresh rosemary or 2 ml ($\frac{1}{2}$ teaspoon) dried
2 ml ($\frac{1}{2}$ teaspoon) ground ginger

Drain apricots and place in a bowl with all remaining ingredie Blend together thoroughly to form soft, chunky mixture.

(Makes 500 ml)

aked bananas with rum sauce

ipe, but firm, bananas in their skins

uce

) ml (1 cup) evaporated milk

-12 soft caramels

ml (4 tablespoons) dark rum

l banana skins well, and grill over moderate coals for about 25 to 30
nutes, turning often until cooked. Skins will blacken, but this does
t mean that the bananas are burning, and you can quite safely keep
em warm around the edge of the fire until required. To make the
uce, place evaporated milk and caramels in a saucepan and heat
rough, stirring occasionally. When caramels have melted, stir in
m, and simmer gently for a few minutes. Serve the sauce either hot
cold with the braaied bananas.

HINTS

*You will make your task a lot lighter if you prepare the sauce and sambals
aead of time.*
*The spicy peanut sauce can be stored, covered, for up to a week in the
frigerator. It is delicious with crudités.*

Butterflied lamb

A buttermilk marinade lends a delicate flavour to braaied lamb, which is complemented by a delicious ratatouille salad, herbed whole mushrooms and garlic baked potatoes.

MENU *Serves six to eight*

Butterflied leg of lamb in buttermilk marinade
Ratatouille salad
Herbed stuffed mushrooms
Baked potatoes with garlic butter

Butterflied leg of lamb in buttermilk marinade

2,5 kg leg of lamb
Buttermilk marinade
2 cloves garlic, crushed
5 ml (1 teaspoon) finely chopped fresh thyme or 2 ml (½ teaspoon) dried
5 ml (1 teaspoon) finely chopped fresh oregano or 2 ml (½ teaspoon) dried
250 ml (1 cup) buttermilk
30 ml (2 tablespoons) lemon juice
2 ml (½ teaspoon) salt
2 ml (½ teaspoon) freshly ground black pepper

Debone the meat and spread it flat. Combine all marinade ingredients and pour into a flat baking dish. Add the meat and marinate for 8 to 12 hours, turning occasionally. Drain and reserve marinade. Braai over hot coals for about 30 to 40 minutes or until tender and succulent, turning and basting regularly with the reserved marinade. Serve the meat slightly pink on the inside; avoid overcooking, as this will dry it out.

VARIATION
A leg of young springbok can be substituted for the lamb.

Ratatouille salad

20 ml (4 teaspoons) olive or sunflower oil
3 medium onions, chopped
2 cloves garlic, crushed
6 baby marrows, thickly sliced
3 medium brinjals, cubed
3 green peppers, seeded and chopped
100 g black olives (optional)
2 bay leaves
5 ml (1 teaspoon) finely chopped fresh thyme or 2 ml (½ teaspoon) dried
15 ml (1 tablespoon) finely chopped fresh basil or 7 ml (1½ teaspoons) dried
625 ml (2½ cups) tomato juice
salt and freshly ground black pepper to taste
fresh parsley, finely chopped

Heat oil in a saucepan and sauté onion until transparent, about 5 minutes. Add all remaining ingredients, except parsley, cover with lid and simmer for about 30 minutes. Allow to cool, then chill overnight in the refrigerator. Serve garnished with chopped parsley.

Herbed stuffed mushrooms

8 large brown mushrooms, stalks removed
Herb stuffing
250 ml (1 cup) cooked brown rice
1 small onion, chopped
30 ml (2 tablespoons) finely chopped fresh parsley
2 ml (½ teaspoon) finely chopped fresh thyme or 1 ml (¼ teaspoon) dried
2 ml (½ teaspoon) finely chopped fresh sage or 1 ml (¼ teaspoon) dried
60 ml (4 tablespoons) natural yoghurt

Mix together all ingredients for herb stuffing and divide equally between the 8 mushroom caps. Braai over moderate coals until tender but not too soft, about 10 minutes.

Baked potatoes with garlic butter

Scrub 8 large, blemish-free potatoes under cold running water, pat dry and season with salt. Prick with a fork and wrap each individually in a double layer of foil, shiny side facing inwards. Place potatoes directly in the coals, towards the edges of the fire where it is cooler. Cook for 40 minutes to an hour, depending on size of potatoes. Turn occasionally to ensure even cooking. Serve hot with garlic butter, prepared by mixing 125 g softened butter with 2 cloves crushed garlic.

HINTS
- *Most of the preparation for this menu should be done a day ahead: the meat must marinate for up to 12 hours, and the salad must be chilled overnight.*
- *Ratatouille salad will keep in the refrigerator for up to 3 days.*
- *Remember to start cooking the mushrooms 10 minutes before the meat is ready.*

22

Rack of lamb feast

A deliciously different way to braai lamb, with mouth-watering accompaniments, and rounded off with a tempting marshmallow treat.

(Illustrated on cover)

MENU *Serves six*
Herbed rack of lamb
Tomatoes with basil stuffing
Cheesy stuffed gem squash
Easy beer bread
Toasted marshmallows
with
Rum and raisin sauce

Herbed rack of lamb

6 racks of lamb, each with 3 to 4 chops
10 ml (2 teaspoons) salt
Coating
50 g butter, softened
20 ml (4 teaspoons) fruit chutney
10 ml (2 teaspoons) prepared mustard
2 cloves garlic, crushed
10 ml (2 teaspoons) lemon juice
125 ml (½ cup) dry wholewheat breadcrumbs
30 ml (2 tablespoons) finely chopped fresh oregano or 15 ml (1 tablespoon) dried
30 ml (2 tablespoons) finely chopped fresh thyme or 15 ml (1 tablespoon) dried

Trim excess fat from lamb and sprinkle meat with salt. Place butter, chutney, mustard, garlic and lemon juice in a bowl, mix well and spread evenly over skin of lamb. Coat with breadcrumbs and herbs, pressing them gently onto the meat by hand. Braai lamb over moderate coals until tender, about 25 to 30 minutes.

Tomatoes with basil stuffing

6 ripe, but firm, tomatoes
Basil stuffing
30 ml (2 tablespoons) butter
4 spring onions, chopped
1 clove garlic, crushed
375 ml (1½ cups) fresh breadcrumbs
15 ml (1 tablespoon) finely chopped fresh basil or 7 ml (1½ teaspoons) dried
5 ml (1 teaspoon) salt
15 ml (1 tablespoon) grated Parmesan cheese

Cut tops off tomatoes, scoop out pulp and set aside. Melt butter in a saucepan and sauté onion and garlic until transparent. Add all remaining ingredients, except cheese. Stir in tomato pulp and cook over medium heat for 1 minute. Spoon mixture into tomato cases and sprinkle each with grated cheese. Place on grid and braai over moderate coals until heated through, about 10 minutes.

Cheesy stuffed gem squash

3 gem squash, halved
Cheese stuffing
125 ml (½ cup) pitted and chopped black olives
500 ml (2 cups) fresh breadcrumbs
1 small onion, chopped
250 ml (1 cup) grated Cheddar cheese
5 ml (1 teaspoon) salt

Boil squash in lightly salted water until cooked. Drain well. Mix all stuffing ingredients together in a bowl and pile spoonfuls into squash halves. Place on grid and braai over moderate coals until cheese has melted, about 10 minutes.

Easy beer bread

500 g self-raising flour
5 ml (1 teaspoon) salt
340 ml (1 bottle) beer

Mix flour and salt together in a bowl. Add beer, and mix to a fairly sticky dough. Spoon dough into a well-greased loaf tin and bake at 180 °C for 1 hour, or until bread sounds hollow when tapped.

VARIATION
Mixed herbs or grated cheese can be added to the bread dough for variety.

Toasted marshmallows

1 x 200 g packet marshmallows

Using a fork or skewer, toast marshmallow over moderate coals until lightly brown a crispy on the outside. Dip into heated r and raisin sauce.

VARIATION
Chunks of fresh fruit, such as pineapple and apple small whole fruit – cherries, for instance – can substituted for marshmallows.

Rum and raisin sauce

250 ml (1 cup) chopped seedless raisins
90 ml (6 tablespoons) coarsely chopp walnuts
190 ml (¾ cup) melted honey
60 ml (4 tablespoons) rum

Place all ingredients in a flame-proof c tainer, stir gently and leave to heat throu over the coolest part of the fire.

HINTS
- *It is best to use fresh herbs for the lamb coatin*
- *The bread recipe is the easiest you will ever mak but remember to allow for an hour's cooking tim Rub the bread crust with butter as soon as you ta it out of the oven to prevent it from becoming t hard.*